How To Teach Social Skills
and Plan for Peer Social Interactions

PRO-ED Series on Autism Spectrum Disorders

Edited by Richard L. Simpson

Titles in the Series

How To Develop and Implement Visual Supports

How To Do Discrete Trial Training

How To Do Incidental Teaching

How To Plan a Structured Classroom

How To Support Children with Problem Behavior

How To Teach Social Skills and Plan for Peer Social Interactions

How To Use Augmentative and Alternative Communication

How To Use Joint Action Routines

How To Use Video Modeling

How To Write and Implement Social Scripts

How To Teach Social Skills and Plan for Peer Social Interactions

Janine Peck Stichter

Maureen A. Conroy

8700 Shoal Creek Boulevard
Austin, Texas 78757-6897
800/897-3202 Fax 800/397-7633
www.proedinc.com

An International Publisher

© 2006 by PRO-ED, Inc.
8700 Shoal Creek Boulevard
Austin, Texas 78757-6897
800/897-3202   Fax 800/397-7633
www.proedinc.com

Library of Congress Cataloging-in-Publication Data

Peck Stichter, Janine.
    How to teach social skills and plan for peer social interactions / Janine Peck
Stichter and Maureen A. Conroy.
       p. cm. — (PRO-ED series on autism spectrum disorders)
    Includes bibliographical references.
    ISBN 1-4164-0149-0 (softcover : alk. paper)
    1. Autistic children.   2. Autism in children.   3. Asperger's syndrome.
  4. Social skills in children.   I. Conroy, Maureen A.   II. Title.   III. Series.
RJ506.A9P43 2006
618.92'85882—dc22

                                                         2005015970

Art Director: Jason Crosier
Designer: Nancy McKinney-Point
This book is designed in Nexus Serif TF and Neutra Text.

Printed in the United States of America

1 2 3 4 5 6 7 8 9 10   09 08 07 06 05

Contents

Contents

From the Editor

About Autism Spectrum Disorders

Autism spectrum disorders (ASD) are complex, neurologically based developmental disabilities that typically appear early in life. The Autism Society of America (2004) estimates that as many as 1.5 million people in the United States have autism or some form of pervasive developmental disorder. Indeed, its prevalence makes ASD an increasingly common and currently the fastest growing developmental disability. ASD are perplexing and enigmatic. According to the *Diagnostic and Statistical Manual of Mental Disorders,* individuals with ASD have difficulty in interacting normally with others; exhibit speech, language, and communication difficulties (e.g., delayed speech, echolalia); insist on routines and environmental uniformity; engage in self-stimulatory and stereotypic behaviors; and respond atypically to sensory stimuli (American Psychiatric Association, 2000; Simpson & Myles, 1998). In some cases, aggressive and self-injurious behavior may be present in these individuals. Yet, in tandem with these characteristics, children with ASD often have normal patterns of physical growth and development, a wide range of cognitive and language capabilities, and some individuals with ASD have highly developed and unique abilities (Klin, Volkmar, & Sparrow, 2000). These widely varied characteristics necessitate specially designed interventions and strategies orchestrated by knowledgeable and skilled professionals.

Preface to the Series

Teaching and managing learners with ASD can be demanding, but favorable outcomes for children and youth with autism and autism-related disabilities depend on professionals using appropriate and valid methods in their education. Because identifying and correctly using effective teaching methods is often enormously challenging (National Research Council, 2001; Simpson et al., 2005), it is the intent of this series to provide professionals with scientifically based methods for intervention. Each book in the series is designed to assist professionals and parents in choosing and correctly using a variety of interventions that have the potential to produce significant benefits for children and youth with ASD. Written in a user-friendly, straightforward fashion by qualified and experienced professionals, the books are aimed at individuals who seek practical solutions and strategies for successfully working with learners with ASD.

Richard L. Simpson
Series Editor

References

American Psychiatric Association. (2000). *Diagnostic and statistical manual of mental disorders* (4th ed., text rev.). Washington, DC: Author.

Autism Society of America. (2004). *What is autism?* Retrieved March 11, 2005, from http://autism-society.org

Klin, A., Volkmar, F., & Sparrow, S. (2000). *Asperger syndrome.* New York: Guilford Press.

National Research Council. (2001). *Educating children with autism.* Committee on Educational Interventions for Children with Autism, Division of Behavioral and Social Sciences and Education. Washington, DC: National Academy Press.

Simpson, R., de Boer-Ott, S., Griswold, D., Myles, B., Byrd, S., Ganz, J., et al. (2005). *Autism spectrum disorders: Interventions and treatments for children and youth.* Thousand Oaks, CA: Corwin Press.

Simpson, R. L., & Myles, B. S. (1998). *Educating children and youth with autism: Strategies for effective practice.* Austin, TX: PRO-ED.

Introduction

Most educators who work with children and youth with autism spectrum disorders (ASD) are aware of their students' social competence difficulties. Indeed, most individuals with ASD lack the social interaction skills needed to develop and maintain friendships with their peers. Children and youth with autism are socially withdrawn, and they rarely engage in appropriate social interactions with their peers. In addition, when peers initiate social interactions, students with ASD frequently fail to respond. Thus, students with ASD are often socially isolated in educational settings. It is not unusual for these students to spend recess time or other social activity times by themselves.

Another factor contributing to the social isolation among students with ASD is their demonstration of unusual behaviors that may interfere with social interactions. Children and youth with ASD may engage in high rates of repetitive behaviors, such as stereotypy and echolalia, and engagement with restricted interests. For example, a young child with ASD may choose to spend the majority of free time spinning the wheels on a toy car, rather than playing functionally with the toy cars and other children. Likewise, an older student with ASD may repeatedly discuss a topic of interest, such as the color and features of cars or lawn mowers. Due to their intense and bizarre nature, these behaviors contribute to the isolation of students with ASD. Researchers have confirmed these observations, reporting that as children with ASD are increasingly included in general education classrooms, their peer-related social skill deficits become more evident, resulting in isolation and peer rejection (Odom, Zercher, Li, Marquart, & Sandall, 2004). Therefore, the development of peer-related social skills among children and youth with ASD needs to be a primary intervention goal. The purpose of this booklet is to provide a systematic process for educators to

Note. Development of this text was partially supported with funding from the U.S. Department of Education, Office of Special Education and Rehabilitative Services (No. H32D990024) and U.S. Department of Education, Office of Special Education Programs, Center on Evidence-Based Practices: Young Children with Challenging Behavior (No. H324Z010001). The opinions expressed by the authors do not necessarily reflect the position of or are endorsed by the U.S. Department of Education.

use to assess children's peer-related social behaviors and to develop individualized, functional social skills intervention programs.

First, an overview of social competence and peer-related social behaviors is presented, including a discussion of the importance of social skill development among students with ASD. Next, a functional approach to assessment is described. Finally, evidence-based strategies for developing peer-related social interactions are outlined. The information presented in this booklet is geared for use primarily by teachers and families and is aimed at enhancing the quality and quantity of social interactions of individuals with ASD with their peers across a variety of settings and activities.

What Is Peer-Related Social Competence?

Peer-related social competence is a person's ability to successfully engage in social interactions and relationships with other individuals. Social competence is typically characterized by social interaction behaviors that are reciprocal, appropriate for the context in which they occur, and effective in reaching a social goal (Odom, McConnell, & McEvoy, 1992). The outcome of successful social interaction behaviors is the development and maintenance of peer-related friendships. Socially competent individuals are typified as able to initiate and maintain friendships, interact appropriately with others, and effectively manage difficult situations.

A central feature of social competence is the social impact of a person's behavior, which is determined by peers' impression. Odom and McConnell (1985) defined social competence as "the interpersonal social performance of children with other children or adults as judged by significant social agents in the child's environment" (p. 9). Thus, social competence is developed through critical behaviors such as making eye contact, asking appropriate or relevant questions, giving compliments, responding appropriately when a peer initiates or gives negative feedback, continuing social interactions, and engaging in conversations. Obviously, the importance of these skills differs depending on a person's age and communicative ability. In addition, a highly influential factor of peer-related social interaction skills is the context in which they occur. Social norms vary across settings; therefore, the contexts or settings in which social interactions occur need to be considered when defining and examining peer-related social competence skills. For instance, a 12-year-old child with ASD who has a high level of knowledge about insects may be able to converse appropriately with an entomologist, but the same conversation held with peers is less likely to be perceived as socially appropriate.

One important factor to note is the reciprocal nature of social interactions (Strain & Shores, 1977). That is, both the individual with ASD and his or her peers must exchange social initiations and responses, resulting in sustained social interactions over time. Through these sustained interactions, social competence and, ultimately, friendships evolve. Therefore, it is critical that individuals with ASD and their peers exhibit social initiations and responses. Without reciprocity, social behavior likely will be extinguished for both the person with ASD and his or her peers. Unfortunately, this occurs all too often for children and youth with ASD. Because persons

1

with ASD tend to initiate fewer social interactions with their peers, their peers tend to do the same. In addition, because persons with ASD often fail to respond to peer initiations, these initiations frequently tend to be extinguished (Odom & Strain, 1986). Accordingly, learning basic social initiation and response behaviors is an important part of developing social competence and friendships for children and youth with ASD.

Why Are Peer-Related Social Skills and Social Competence Important?

The impact of peer-related social competence and social interaction deficits on children and youth with ASD cannot be overstated. As many parents will testify, the lack of social networks and friendships among children diagnosed with ASD significantly affects their quality of life. Children and youth with social competence deficits lack friends and spend much of their time socially isolated. For instance, they often have difficulty in dealing with and maintaining relationships, reading social cues, and responding appropriately in different social situations. Social isolation not only negatively effects the quality of students' lives, but also leads to deficits in other developmental skill areas, such as language and cognition (see Bijou, 1976; Vygotsky, 1978).

As more and more children with ASD and other disabilities are educated in inclusive, general education settings, peer-related social competence becomes even more essential. Physically including children with ASD in general education classrooms is not sufficient; social competence and inclusion is even more important. To ensure social inclusion for students with ASD, teachers must target peer-related social interaction skills for intervention. Lifelong friendships often begin in school settings. And without early development of social competence, the outlook for social inclusion for children with ASD beyond school years is dismal. Social competence deficits will affect these individuals' abilities to obtain employment and participate in community activities as adults. It is not unusual for persons with ASD to be successful in completing work-related tasks (e.g., filing books in a library, entering data into a computer), but at the same time, have difficulty adapting to their work environment or interacting with others in that environment. In fact, this lack of social skills can result in loss of employment. Hence, instruction in peer-related social skills should be primary components of the curriculum and educational plans for children and youth with ASD, beginning in the early years and continuing through high school. The first step to developing a social skills curriculum is to conduct a thorough assessment. In the next section, a functional approach to assessment of peer-related social skills for students with ASD is outlined.

Functional Assessment of Peer-Related Social Skills

To obtain an accurate representation of student's peer-related social strengths and weaknesses, teachers need to observe and evaluate social behaviors in the natural settings in which they occur, including classrooms, schools, and the community. In addition to assessing students' social behaviors in these environments, teachers should also assess the social demands of these settings and the social behaviors of peers. In this section, we describe a functional assessment process that teachers can use to identify peer-related social interaction skills and abilities to target for instruction.

Typically, when a student has an identified deficit, formal assessment strategies are used to evaluate skill levels. In the area of peer-related social skills, however, there are few formalized or standardized assessments available. In addition, the standardized assessment tools that are available do not specifically address the idiosyncratic features of social deficits demonstrated by many individuals with ASD. As a result, the assessment of peer-related social skills in children with ASD involves using multiple methods across multiple settings (Odom & McConnell, 1985). The assessment process described in this section provides a framework for assessing several critical dimensions of peer-related social behaviors using multiple tools and strategies across environments. Use of this comprehensive assessment process leads to a thorough understanding of a child's peer-related social behaviors across a variety of contexts.

Step 1: Assessing the Form of Social Skills

A good beginning point for an assessment is to identify the critical peer-related social behaviors. Figure 1 presents an assortment of peer-related, initiation and response behaviors that are vital for the development of social competence (Conroy & Brown, 2002).

A social initiation is typically defined as a social bid directed from one person to another person to begin a social interaction (Odom, McConnell, & McEvoy, 1992). Social initiations may include different forms of behavior, including verbal, gestural, and motoric. For example, a child may indicate a desire to play with another child by calling the child's name and asking to

Helping, showing affection, or comforting

Commenting

Organizing a social activity

Greeting

Maintaining a conversation

Repeating what others say

Clarifying a peer's comments

Establishing eye contact

Establishing joint attention

Requesting information or assistance from peers

Complimenting peers

Providing information to peers

Responding to peers' initiations

FIGURE 1. Peer-related social interaction behaviors vital for the development of social competence.

play (verbal), waving at the child to come over to the play area (gestural), or pulling the child's hand toward the play area (motoric). An initiation will typically be followed by a response which may be verbal, gestural, or motoric. For example, if a child asks another child to play, the second child may respond by saying, "Yes, that sounds fun" (verbal), shaking his or her head "yes" and smiling (gestural), or just joining the play activity (motoric). What happens after the initial initiation–response sequence is also important. Often, a social interaction or a series of related social behaviors follow the initial initiation–response sequence. These subsequent interactions also include verbal, gestural, and motoric behaviors, such as sharing materials, assisting a person, communicating information, engaging in a conversation, showing affection toward another, and playing a game.

Children and youth with ASD frequently have difficulty initiating, responding to, and maintaining social interactions. Occasionally, they may even engage in inappropriate social behaviors (e.g., show aggression toward a peer as a means of indicating refusal to play). Thus, social interactions occur less frequently among children with ASD, resulting in fewer opportunities to develop peer-related friendships.

Step 2: Assessing the Function of Socials Skills

In addition to assessing the form of social behaviors, it is also important to assess the purpose or function of these behaviors. If, for example, a child asks another child to share his GameBoy, a teacher needs to consider the reason behind the initiation. Does the child want the other child's attention or is he more interested in obtaining the GameBoy (i.e., a tangible item)? In another situation, a child might push away another child who approaches him to play. The purpose of that behavior may be a desire to play alone, that is, escape a social interaction. Some of the reasons persons may engage in peer-related initiations and responses include (a) to gain peer attention, (b) to escape peer attention, (c) to obtain a tangible item or activity, or (d) to escape a tangible item or activity. Identifying the purpose or function of an individual's social behaviors is integral to developing suitable interventions. The *Social Skills Interview* (SSI; Asmus, Conroy, Ladwig, Boyd, & Sellers, 2004) and the *Snapshot Assessment Tool* (SAT; Conroy, Asmus, Ladwig, Sellers, & Boyd, 2004) are two informal assessment instruments designed to assess peer-related social skills of children with ASD. The SSI is an indirect measure that examines a number of factors related to social skills, including (a) the child's current social behaviors and communication strategies (both appropriate and inappropriate), (b) opportunities for social interactions, (c) events that are likely to predict social behaviors, and (d) factors that may maintain social behaviors. The SSI was designed to be used as an interview tool and can be completed by a variety of persons, including classroom teachers and family members who have had opportunities to observe a child in many social situations.

Outcomes of the SSI can help teachers target intervention goals and strategies. A copy of the SSI can be found in Appendix A, where it has been completed for a student named Garrison. Garrison is able to engage in peer-related social interactions; however, he rarely initiates to his peers unless an adult prompts him. When he does initiate, he uses short phrases and gestures, and these initiations typically occur during recess, lunch, and music. He is less likely to initiate during large group or noisy activities. Garrison is most likely to play with friends Michael and Roberto at school, and is more likely to engage in peer-related social interactions when an adult is present and prompting him. In addition, he is more likely to engage in social interactions if he is playing in a small group with materials that interest him. Garrison usually initiates to his peers to obtain a play item that he wants (e.g., a book, the computer).

The *Snapshot Assessment Tool* (SAT) is a direct-observation tool designed to capture a "snapshot" of the child's peer-related social behaviors across a variety of settings. By conducting several observations using the SAT, teachers can obtain a representative sample of the form and function of children's initiation and response behaviors, the context in which those behaviors occur, the reciprocity of the social exchange, and the perceived goals and actual outcomes of the exchange. A copy of the SAT can be found in Appendix B, where it has been completed for Garrison. When using the SAT, teachers should observe the child in five different activities when he or she is engaged in peer-related social behaviors. Although children with ASD typically exhibit low rates of peer-related social behavior, they are likely to engage in social behavior during some activities throughout the day. These activities can be identified through the SSI or a teacher's or parent's report. By observing several of the child's peer-related social interactions, the teacher may be able to identify a pattern. For example, the SAT shown in Appendix B illustrates that peer-related social initiations with Garrison typically do not result in interaction. That is, when Garrison initiates, peers often do not respond, and when peers initiate to Garrison, he often does not respond. Therefore, Garrison's peer-related social interactions lack reciprocity. Garrison appears to engage in peer-related social behaviors to obtain tangible items and peer attention, as well as escape peer attention. He appears to be successful more often than not in meeting his social goals. The SAT in Appendix B represents just one observation of Garrison's peer-related social behaviors. To obtain a more representative sample, a teacher should observe Garrison over several days and activities.

Although the SSI and SAT were developed for younger children with ASD, teachers may want to adapt them for older students. Adaptations may include the activities or contexts of social interaction opportunities and types of social interaction behaviors. For example, rather than looking at early childhood play activities, such as housekeeping or dramatic play, teachers would observe typical activities of older children, such as recess, and before-school and after-school activities. Regardless of the assessment procedures employed, teachers will want to obtain a representative sample of the student's peer-related social abilities using several techniques across a variety of settings.

Step 3: Assessing the Social Contexts

In addition to assessing the form and function of peer-related social skills, teachers will want to consider the social contexts in which those skills occur. Evaluating the social context involves assessing the availability and social skills of the peers in the student's classroom, school, or community. Because there is no formal instrument available to assess the social context, teachers will need to informally assess it by asking the following questions:

- Are there peers available for interactions?
- If so, do they interact with the child with ASD?

- Do the peers have the social abilities to interact with the child with ASD?
- Do the peers persist in interacting if the child with ASD does not respond?
- Do the peers respond appropriately to the child's initiations?
- Are the peers interested in interacting with the child with ASD?

Step 4: Assessing the Physical Contexts

Next, teachers need to evaluate the social requirements of the classroom, school, or community in which the student with ASD functions. This is equally important for facilitating successful inclusion in these settings. In school, for example, there are a number of social expectations throughout the day. When children enter the classroom, they are expected to greet the teacher as well as each other. In the lunchroom, they are expected to wait in line, take turns, ask for food, or request assistance if needed. During the day in the classroom, they are expected to wait their turn, share materials, attend to others through eye contact and body orientation, and refrain from engaging in disruptive behaviors. Although many of these behaviors may be applied across settings, each setting or activity has its own social expectations. Once again, there is no standardized assessment designed for assessing social requirements and opportunities within contexts. Therefore, teachers will want to conduct their own informal evaluations of the student's settings, which will help the teacher identify the skills required to function in the settings and target skills for instruction. Moreover, when children and youth are taught the skills required to be successful in a particular setting or activity, they are more likely to flourish in that setting. Factors for teachers to consider when evaluating the social expectations of a setting include the following:

- What activities take place in the setting?
- Who participates in those activities?
- What are the social expectations of those activities?
- What social skills are required for students to be successful in those activities?
- How do the target child's social skills compare to those that are required for those activities?
- What social skills does the child need to learn to participate in those activities?

As children and youth with ASD progress into secondary education and spend additional time in the community, teachers become increasingly responsible for assessment of the social ability of their students across settings. Although teachers may be familiar with these community environments, it can be more difficult to recognize idiosyncratic differences in the social interactions of the child with ASD across contexts. In these instances, as well as in more complicated scenarios within educational settings, a discrepancy analysis form can be used as a more systematic way to respond to the questions listed above. As an example, Table 1 compares the social and functional expectations of going to a movie with current functioning of a teenager with ASD.

TABLE 1
Discrepancy Analysis

Environment: Movie theater complex

Subenvironment: Ticket line and concession area

Activity: Buying tickets and food for a movie

Inventory of Nondisabled Student	Inventory of Student with ASD	Skills or Areas that Student with ASD Needs Adapted or Accommodated
1. Stands in front of box office and looks up to choose movie	1. Stands in front of doors looking around, appears overstimulated (e.g., good deal of body rocking)	1. Student sits with friend and newspaper prior to leaving and chooses movie; student picks alternative in case it's sold out
2. Looks for and approaches correct line to purchase ticket	2. Goes up to closest line when prompted to "Get your ticket"	2. Friend shows student line in which to stand
3. Waits in line	3. Paces back and forth next to the line	3. Student talks with friend about how long it will take to go through line and reviews social story
4. Requests number of tickets and pays for them	4. Stares at box office attendant, has no functional communication	4. Student uses prewritten cue card to request ticket and predetermined amount of money to pay
5. Approaches ticket taker, gives ticket, waits for stub	5. Tries to walk past ticket taker	5. Friend models behavior
6. Goes to concession area and waits in line	6. Goes straight to concession area and looks at candy behind the glass	6. Student and friend predetermine desired snack and amount of money needed
7. Decides what to order	7. Points repeatedly at candy, not indicating preference	7. Student signs "help" to friend if needed
8. Asks for and purchases desired items	8. Waits for someone to buy the candy	

Analyzing Assessment Results and Identifying Target Goals for Intervention

Peer-related social skills depend on the context in which they occur. Accordingly, it is important for teachers not only to assess the target child's peer-related social skills but also the child's social and physical opportunities for peer-related social interactions. Because of the lack of standardized assessment instruments, teachers must adapt informal assessment tools, like the ones mentioned in this manual, for their own use and even consider developing additional teacher-made tools to assist in the identification of target skills for instruction.

Once target peer-related social skills and opportunities for teaching those goals have been assessed, teachers will need to analyze their assessment results to identify skills to target for intervention. Teachers can compare the social demands of the environment to the child's social abilities to identify emerging functional social skills that can be used across a variety of settings. The following questions will help teachers determine the course of instruction. Identify variables to target for instruction by asking the following questions:

- What skills need to be taught or adapted to facilitate social inclusion of the child?
- Will these skills help the child function more independently in his or her environment?
- Is there a need to rearrange the environment to facilitate more opportunities for social interactions?
- Do peers need to learn new social interaction skills?

By analyzing the discrepancies between the social requirements of the child's environment and the child's peer-related social skills, teachers can develop an effective intervention plan. In the next section, we outline strategies for facilitating peer-related social behaviors in children with ASD.

Once the priorities for social skill instruction have been determined for a child through systematic assessment, the next logical step is to determine the type and delivery method of instruction. When the significant implications of poor social skills are weighed against the degree to which children and youth with ASD are typically challenged in this area, it becomes quite evident why an integrated and planned social skills curriculum is necessary for these individuals. In addition, given the learning characteristics of students with ASD (i.e., poor skill generalization and maintenance), the focus of any curriculum requires that there be a clear framework for the delivery of instruction within natural social contexts and natural social agents (i.e., peers) to the degree appropriate. The match between a child's social profiles and the strategies used should reflect a continuum of intervention and appropriate environments. Therefore, it is essential to be able to identify what combination of environments and levels of instruction along this continuum are most appropriate toward developing social competence across targeted areas of functioning and interaction. To assist teachers in accomplishing this, Brown and colleagues developed a model that presents a hierarchy of levels of interventions that promote peer-related social competence (Brown, Odom, & Conroy, 2001). The remainder of this section will be organized around key components of this model, allowing for presentation of various strategies representing a continuum of intensity and support based on the student's individual level of need.

Using Integrated Environments To Promote Peer-Based Social Competence

Before an appropriate intervention can be chosen for a child, a teacher must determine the source of a particular social deficit, particularly whether it is the result of the following (Snell & Janney, 2000): (a) an acquisition problem (i.e., the child lacks the skill); (b) a performance or fluency problem (i.e., the child has the skill, but may not know when to use it, may use it too slowly, or may be unable to modify it in different situations); or

(c) interfering or competing behaviors (i.e., the child has key or numerous other behaviors that interfere with the demonstration of the social skill).

The type of deficit will determine the intervention strategy and level of intensity. Consider the case of Julia. Julia is able to successfully take turns while playing checkers at home with her father, yet while playing basketball on the playground, a less structured activity, she is always yelled at for "hogging the ball." Although Julia may know the rules of the game, she is still an unpopular participant, if allowed to join at all, because she does not share the ball. Julia's assessment indicates that she has a performance deficit in knowing when to take turns, particularly during less structured activities with peers. Likely, the best support for this type of performance deficit would be for Julia to continue participating in activities with her peers in naturally occurring situations, as opposed to a one-on-one session with a counselor away from the very activities that create the challenge for her. On the other hand, if her skill deficit was one of fluency, she would need ongoing opportunities to practice. Because Julia is having difficulty recognizing when to use the rules she knows in certain situations, those same situations are a required backdrop for any level of instruction from which she would benefit. Peers are often used in a one-on-one or small-group format to address problems of skill acquisition. In these situations, peers can be provided with specific cues and strategies for engaging the target student appropriately. When full skill acquisition does not appear, peers may also assist the target student with the use of adaptations (e.g., the use of a picture cue card to indicate a desire to play). Additional self-management and adult-supported strategies for use in the context of peer interactions will be discussed further in subsequent sections. In all of these cases, inclusive social environments serve as the natural teaching platform, with or without additional strategies.

If, however, Julia has been in this setting for quite some time and has had multiple opportunities to practice (i.e., peers have allowed her to participate), then she will require supplementary strategies to help her acquire fluency in turn taking or to provide her with specific tools to identify when and where to use the skills she has already learned (e.g., wait until the ball is passed to her as opposed to grabbing it from a team member). Such strategies seem particularly necessary for children and youth with ASD who tend to have difficulty fully assessing social nuances and unstructured activities. These students find it especially challenging to determine when to use or modify specific skills, especially with peers, who tend to be less predictable than adults in their requests and reactions. Such strategies—including social reading techniques and performance feedback strategies—will enhance the benefits of naturally occurring situations in fully inclusive contexts. It is important to note that any of these strategies can be used across all levels of instruction. We simply list them here as examples of typical interventions for this degree of need.

Social Reading Techniques

Social reading techniques use situations from a child's actual experience to visually present social information and teach social competence. *Social scripts* and *social stories* show individuals how to employ a combination of social skills within naturally occurring situations (Gray, 1994; Scott, Clark, & Brady, 2000). Social scripts are usually composed of targeted, short phrases or a set of behaviors that an individual employs under a specific condition. Social stories, on the other hand, tend to be longer than scripts and have specific guidelines for composition (see Gray, 1994). Figures 2a and 2b show examples of each. Typically written by parents, professionals, or even peers, these scripts and stories describe social situations and are frequently used to reduce child fear, to teach good judgment, to teach social skills, and to ease child transition.

When used with students who can read, the social story or script is written using descriptive sentences that provide contextual cues (e.g., When someone comes up to you and says, "Hi, Tom!") for a directed behavior (e.g., You should say, "Hi!" back to the person *before* you walk away). When used with individuals who are unable to read, the story or script employs icons to visually describe the sequence. In either form, social scripts and stories capitalize on a typical strength of individuals with ASD, visual processing, while providing structure to an often unpredictable social situation (e.g.,

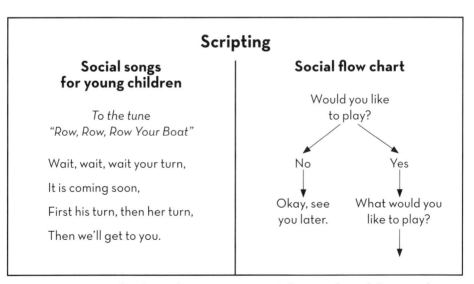

FIGURE 2a. Example of social scripts. *Note.* Social song adapted from *Students with Autism: Characteristics and Instructional Programming for Special Educators,* by J. Scott, C. Clark, and M. Brady, 2000, San Diego, CA: Singular.

Fire Drills

Sometimes we are surprised with fire drills at school. It is important to have fire drills so we can practice what to do in case there is a real fire. First we hear the bell ring. It is very loud. I want to cover my ears and yell, "Stop," but I don't. I tell myself that the bell will stop pretty soon and I take a deep breath. All of the kids get in line and walk quickly down the hall. We have to stay in line when we are outside so the teacher can make sure everyone is there. The teacher will tell me when it is time to go back into the school.

FIGURE 2b. Example of a social story.

responding to greetings and questions at the lunch table). Another benefit of social stories and scripts is that they help ensure that adults at home as well as school are prompting children and youth with ASD similarly for desired behavior.

To create social script and stories, teachers should ask children's peers for help because they typically have the best pulse on the social norms and nuances that would most enhance peer-based social competence. When learning social scripts or stories, children will typically refer to them frequently to memorize their components and even role-play when appropriate. As the children become more fluent in their application of skills, they may refer to the scripts and stories less often.

Performance Feedback

Another strategy that capitalizes on naturally occurring situations is *performance feedback.* Hopefully available in numerous ways for all children during their school day, performance feedback typically is given in the form of such things as rewards and encouragement throughout the day. For the purpose of this booklet, performance feedback refers to a more directed form of feedback, provided when a student encounters a social situation in which he or she exhibits certain social skills, but the outcome is not a successful social interaction. Consider the following scenario:

A group of girls are reading a magazine during study hall. Teresa loves magazines and wants to see what the girls are doing. She has learned not to just grab the magazine, but instead knows she should approach the group, greet them, and then ask about their activity. When she does this, however, she interrupts two of the girls speaking with her loud greeting, then asks them what they are doing. Unfortunately, Teresa does not wait for an answer; instead, she comments on how many magazines she has read and says that her favorite color is red so she really likes magazines with red sweaters in them. She continues rambling, asking whether their magazine has red sweaters in it. The other girls tolerate the interaction for a short time and then tell her they will bring her the magazine at her table when they are done.

In this scenario Teresa has executed the correct sequence of skills for initiating and demonstrating a shared interest. However, she has broken almost all four Maxims of Conversation Interaction (Grice, 1975). Grice described these as follows:

1. Quantity—be informative but not verbose. Teresa spoke non-stop about red sweaters and enjoyment of magazines without recognizing social discomfort of others.
2. Quality—be honest, or be truthful to the topic. Teresa filled in a knowledge gap about exactly what kind of magazine the other girls were looking at by assuming that the magazine would or should be one that has a lot of red sweaters.
3. Relevance—stay true to the topic. Teresa talked about how many magazines she had read and her preference for red sweaters in magazines instead of commenting on the MP3 players pictured on the page of the magazine about which the girls were speaking.
4. Clarity—ensure the message is clear to the listener. The girls were not sure why Teresa was telling them about red sweaters or her magazine collection.

Problems with any or all of these four maxims are most evident for children who have some form of performance deficit. They have already mastered skill acquisition; the application is what is more challenging for them. Feedback on any of these four maxims is easily provided in natural settings by both adults and peers, and is essential for the development of successful social interactions. If feedback is provided outside a natural social interaction environment, then it is too far removed and distant to be useful. Feedback can be given verbally in the context of the interactions; typically socially competent individuals receive such feedback when their peers gently suggest that they are telling "fish tales" (i.e., quantity), or ask with a smile, "And so ... what's your point?" (i.e., clarity). For children and youth with ASD, the prompts may need to be more direct (e.g., "That's interesting, but we are talking about MP3 players. Do you have one?") and consistent. These are examples of how peers and even adults can develop with relative ease key words to prompt children in specific areas of challenges.

For children and youth that need a little more concrete explanation and correction on problem interaction, a *social autopsy* might be desirable (Myles & Simpson, 2001). Social autopsies are a way of reviewing a previous social interaction and identifying its strengths and weaknesses (see Appendix C). By using categories such as the four Maxims of Conversation Interaction, or other categories as predetermined with the child, the child can work with a peer, adult, or him- or herself to diagnose specific problems to work on for the next interaction. Once they can identify specific areas of need, the student can use self-management techniques such as developing a social story or reviewing a mental or physical checklist.

Adapting the Environment
To Promote Social Competence

Simply encouraging and reflecting on social interactions within natural contexts may often be insufficient for many children and youth with ASD to develop peer-related social competence. This may be because naturally occurring opportunities for the desired social interaction (e.g., greetings, asking someone about mutual interests) may not occur within the target environment frequently enough to provide sufficient opportunities for practice. Other times, children may need a structured situation in which to work on one aspect of an interaction with ongoing support before demonstrating social competence in a natural setting. Environmental modifications may include seating certain individuals together for activities or planning specific opportunities for a child to use a skill (e.g., a computer game that requires turn taking).

Incidental Teaching

One way to provide structured learning opportunities in a natural environment is through *incidental teaching,* a technique that capitalizes on a person's interests and natural motivation. As in more traditional teacher-directed instruction, incidental teaching is planned and can be used in an instructional curriculum for children and youth with ASD. But what makes incidental teaching unique is its focus on *student*-directed teaching, that is, following the student's lead regarding interests within naturally occurring daily activities. Because children and youth with ASD often do not maintain interest in teacher- or peer-led activities, this method suits them particularly well. Most teachers use "teachable moments" throughout the day with their students, asking them, for example, to make requests and choices in the classroom or identify the type of animal found in a book a student recently checked out of the library. Incidental teaching involves being planful in using teachable moments initiated by the student. Daily routines that can be used for teaching include eating meals, using learning centers, passing out papers for a project to peers, playing, taking car trips, watching movies, listening to music, as well as performing functional or academic tasks. By planning in advance about how these daily routines may be expanded as the child initiates interests, the teacher can best optimize these opportunities for instruction.

Because incidental teaching is planned, the teacher can identify key instructional goals, which will help the teacher determine key peer-related activities and teachable moments. Once these types of opportunities have been determined, there are four levels of prompts that a teacher or peer can use.

Level 1: At this level, the teacher waits 30 seconds, or a similar time period, before prompting a child when the child shows interest in an object or is close to a potential initiation with another child. The goal is for the child to verbally initiate for the object during the delay. For example, if a child with ASD approaches a child doing a dinosaur puzzle, the teacher waits 30 seconds before prompting an initiation from the child with ASD.

Level 2: After 30 seconds (or other predetermined short duration), if the child has not verbally requested or referenced the activity, then the teacher prompts the appropriate verbalization (e.g., "What do you want to do?").

Level 3: If the child does not respond to the Level 2 prompt, then the teacher provides a more specific prompt while showing the desired object (e.g., "Do you want to help Jim finish the puzzle?").

Level 4: At this level, the most intense, the child is prompted to imitate the appropriate verbalization as modeled by the teacher or peer (e.g., "Can I play?").

Teachers should use the least intense level of prompt possible to encourage the response. Once the child responds appropriately, the teacher should confirm the child's response by reacting to the request, giving praise, or expanding a phrase ("Dominoes? You want to play dominoes?") that becomes the natural consequence or reinforcer.

During the use of incidental teaching, we strongly suggest that the teacher collect observational data to assess the child's present starting skill levels and to track ongoing progress, while making any necessary adjustments. Once initial levels of responses are achieved, the prompting hierarchy can be used to gain more elaborate responses. Incidental teaching can be used with students at all levels of communication and social competence. This flexible process can be tailored to elicit very basic initiations or responses, or to foster more complex social interactions. Figure 3 lists several tips and examples for successful use of incidental teaching.

Cooperative Learning Groups

Using key principles of incidental teaching, *cooperative learning groups* are another means for creating or modifying the instructional environment to facilitate reciprocal peer interactions. Students with ASD may work well in cooperative learning groups because these students frequently prefer situations with structure, rules, and consistency, and these groups, by their nature, have a common purpose, a basic set of materials and governing requirements, and various roles that can be assigned. Cooperative learning groups can promote social competence as well as deliver academic and functional curricula, and groups are typically divided into five types, each with a different social goal. Cooperative learning group goals should be matched to the identified social competence goals to develop learning environments that best support desired social, as well as academic, outcomes. The five groups and strategies for promoting social skills in each are discussed next.

1. **Positive Interdependence/Group Goal.** Goals are structured to promote accomplishments and success for all group members.

Strategies:
- Structure assignments so job cannot be completed unless all team members participate.
- Organize materials and structure responding for group participation (e.g., team members develop group goals collaboratively, one pencil for recorder, one paper submitted by group).
- Provide reinforcement to all group members for meeting group goals.

2. **Individual Accountability.** Each student's mastery of the assigned content is assessed.

Strategies:
- Provide rewards and bonus points for individual improvement or progress.

Tips for Effective Use of Incidental Teaching

- **Give yourself and the child time.** It is hard to attend to child initiations if you are always in a rush.

- **Use incidental teaching to develop language and social skills when the child wants something such as food, an activity, a toy, attention, or help.** In this case, be sure to give the child what he or she asks for. If you are encouraging language use, and the child asks for a ball, you will naturally reinforce the child's use of language by giving the item requested (i.e., the ball). The child will learn that using communication skills gets him or her what he or she wants.

- **Recognize that elaboration of child's skills is an important part of incidental teaching.** Support the child in giving an elaborated response. By providing models of responses and questioning the child, the teacher helps the child learn.

- **Keep incidental teaching relatively brief and enjoyable.** If a situation becomes lengthy or unpleasant, stop and redirect to another activity.

- **Preplan.** Incidental teaching, although natural, is not happenstance. Take time to plan the times during the day when you will use incidental teaching. For example, if your students are going on a community outing, think about how you can teach language and concepts during this time (e.g., color and object identification, social greetings).

- **Start small and set goals.** For example, in the beginning, you might say, "Today I will identify three or four teachable moments and use them." As you practice incidental teaching, set your goals a little higher. If used regularly, incidental teaching will become more natural, but you should still plan ahead to ensure you will meet instructional goals.

- **Encourage and teach others to use incidental teaching.** Others who may benefit include paraprofessional staff, immediate and extended family members, and older children.

(continues)

FIGURE 3. Using incidental teaching effectively.

Example of Incidental Teaching

While Mario was playing with a toy car, Kyle tried to grab it from him. Mrs. Perkins put her hand over Kyle's on top of the toy and waited, looking expectantly at Kyle. Kyle did not respond. Mrs. Perkins said, "What do you want?" Kyle said, "Car." Mrs. Perkins said, "That's right, car," and asked Mario to choose a toy car to give to Kyle. Mario gave Kyle a red car. Mrs. Perkins said to Kyle, "You have a red car. What color is it?" Kyle said, "Red." Mrs. Perkins said, "Very good. It is red. What color is Mario's car?" Kyle said, "Yellow." Mrs. Perkins said, "Yes, yellow. You and Mario can drive the cars on the mat." The teaching could stop here, or Mrs. Perkins could continue to work with Kyle on colors or on a social interaction if Kyle expressed interest in playing with Mario.

FIGURE 3. *Continued.*

- Conduct random comprehension checks, selecting one group member to respond to questions.
- Require students to check each other's work, and select one paper from the group for review.

3. **Task Specialization.** Students become experts on various aspects of the group assignment.

Strategies:
- Assign a group of "experts" specific sections of content area texts with the task of preparing a study guide to disseminate to the whole class.
- Let students select subtopics of a unit to be compiled by the group.
- Encourage students to select methods of problem solving and responding based on personal strengths (e.g., written, oral, demonstration, art project, video).

4. **Opportunities for Success.** The contributions of all team members are valued.

Strategies:
- Award team points based on improvement of past scores.
- Place students with peers of similar ability in competitive situations (e.g., tournaments or games).

- Ensure that required contributions are appropriate for students' present levels, but value each contribution equally (e.g., 6 math problems completed correctly by student with disability receive same points as 12 for a typical peer).

5. **Face-to-Face Interaction.** Groups are structured to facilitate collaborative efforts.

Strategies:
- Structure the physical arrangement of the classroom to facilitate collaborative efforts (e.g., set up interactive play centers and writing corners that facilitate discussion and creativity).
- Select instructional methods and cooperative goals that encourage interaction (e.g., reciprocal reading and questioning, elaboration, summarizing).
- Award points for demonstration of positive collaborative behaviors.

Play Groups

Similar to cooperative learning groups, *play groups* often serve as environmental modifications for younger children. Typically, the goals of cooperative play groups are more simplistic than those of the aforementioned learning groups, with an emphasis on cooperation, sharing, and turn taking for younger children with ASD. Teachers should note the following key issues when designing play groups to ensure the maximum effect while keeping the group fun and enjoyable for all children:

- Use natural environments where social interactions normally occur.
    a. Make sure activity and play areas are well defined, with at least three borders.
    b. Keep play areas from being overcrowded or having excessive noise.

- Design groups of at least two or three children and no more than five children.
    a. Place children with diverse abilities in each group, but keep in mind that the majority of the children should be socially competent.
    b. Ensure consistency and predictability of social behaviors within the group.
    c. Have the groups meet regularly (e.g., twice a week for 30 min. each).

    d. Use a consistent schedule and routines (e.g., opening and clos-
      ing rituals).

- Use appropriate play materials.

    a. Organize play materials so they are easily accessible (e.g., label
      and place at appropriate level).
    b. Consider the age appropriateness of toys and activities.
    c. Obtain plain and simple toys (except for dress up).

Using Coaching Strategies

Some children and youth with ASD need more specific instruction due to
increased cognitive and social–emotional challenges or because they exhibit skill deficits in one or more areas of a desired interaction sequence
(e.g., they do not seem to recognize when a peer is initiating contact). These
individuals may benefit from coaching strategies such as adult-mediated
instruction and peer-mediated interventions, which provide more direct
instruction. In *adult-mediated instruction,* the teacher or parent prompts
and reinforces appropriate social interactions (Allen, Hart, Buell, Harris,
& Wolf, 1964; Odom & Strain, 1986). Typically, the adult uses a specific set
of verbal statements and physical cues or gestures to prompt the child to
make a targeted social initiation (e.g., assisting, sharing) or to respond to an
initiation by a peer. The adult praises the resulting interaction with verbal
or tangible reinforcement. Because adults are typically in charge of increas-
ing social competence for children and also performing social assessments,
they tend to be rather consistent, and it is easy to teach them proper direct
instruction techniques. However, there are significant drawbacks to relying
too heavily on adult-mediated instruction, including the following:

- Children and youth with ASD may rely solely on adult prompts
  or specific reinforcement to perform desired behavior (e.g., the
  child only initiates when her primary teacher greets her).
- Because children with more significant impairments will gen-
  erally have constant or near-constant adult supervision, fading
  adult prompts and reliance on adults can be quite challenging
  and actually may interfere with peer-related social behaviors.
  Researchers have realized for quite some time that, in these
  cases, fading tends to be lengthy and unlikely in natural settings.
- Teacher praise may be disruptive to ongoing social interaction
  between peers and other adults. The child with ASD may only
  associate with the reinforcement, causing the peer to become
  extraneous to the social situation. Additionally, peers may also

learn to interact with the target students only through the adult rather than directly with students.

In *peer-mediated interventions,* peers are taught by adults specifically to deliver instructional encouragement (Odom & Strain, 1984). Although a teacher may be present and closely monitor the situation, he and she does not intervene directly with the target child. Typical steps of peer-mediated interventions for all ages include the following:

1. Priority interaction skills for students with ASD are identified.
2. Confederate peers are chosen. Research indicates that dyads (one confederate per student with ASD) typically work better than triads (two confederate peers per student with ASD; Sasso, 1989; Sasso, Mundschenk, Melloy, & Casey, 1998).
3. Teachers train confederate peer(s) to direct social initiations to a target student.
4. Confederate peers initiate and lead social interactions in predetermined activities that could occur naturally in current settings.
5. Teachers prompt and reinforce confederate peers for successful attempts.
6. Peers persist in prompting and reinforcing the target student for desired interaction skills.

Some tips for making peer-mediated interventions successful include the following:

- Teachers should create an aura of honor for general education students who are involved in social interaction activities.
- Peer-mediated groups should be kept small in the beginning. More participants can be added later.
- Use of multiple peers can be effective. Initially, peers are taught to interact with target students one on one, demonstrating typical friendship development. Peer networks are formed once additional "friends" are brought into the social interactions.

We have discussed the importance and benefits of using peers to assist in naturally occurring interactions as well as in more structured situations, including incidental teaching, cooperative peer groups, play groups, and adult-mediated instruction or peer-mediated intervention. However, it is essential to recognize that just as parents and teachers often need instruction on the best strategies for supporting social competence, peers need formal instruction as well. As stated previously, peers are a great source for identifying the strengths and needs of target children with ASD for successful interactions in current and future environments. Providing peers with consistent cues, prompts, and reinforcement, as well as appropriate environmental structure assisting peers with ASD, is indeed essential. Table 2 describes key steps in the development and training of peer networks (Garrison-Harrell, Kamps, & Kravitz, 1997; Haring & Breen, 1992).

TABLE 2
Key Activities for Starting Peer Networks

A peer network begins with a group of friends, who are asked to include a new member, a student with ASD. The students in the peer network should understand why they are being asked to include the new student. Researchers and educators alike have found the following activities essential for beginning and maintaining this process (Haring & Breen, 1992).

Understand the value of peer networks	• Quality of life is increased for all students involved. • Social competency is enhanced through peer modeling. • Students have better awareness of disability.
Identify a peer network	• Students share common interests. • Students share classes. • Groups contain four or five students.
Provide adult support	• Adult facilitator is designated. • Primary classroom teacher is involved. • Adult provides structure and consistency. • Adult should be comfortable answering questions and training students on strategies best suited for target child.
Pay attention to setup and monitoring	• Students' and peers' schedules are mapped. • Students are assigned formal times to hang out. • Adult ensures that there are opportunities for the students to see one another during normal routines. • Nondisabled peers are selected to assist in determining preferences and needs. • Group is assisted in deciding what is essential to teach and how best to do so. • Data are recorded on interactions and process.
Attend to times and contexts for interaction	• Peers commit to attend and view as a positive addition to their lives. • Peers commit to be open and honest. • Adults commit to maintaining the structure and routines, to welcoming and supporting peer feedback, to training necessary skills, and to incorporating peer comments and suggestions.

Note. Adapted from "A Peer-Mediated Social Network Intervention To Enhance the Social Integration of Persons with Moderate and Severe Disabilities," by T. G. Haring and C. G. Breen, 1992, *Journal of Applied Behavior Analysis, 25*(2), pp. 319–333.

Matching Instruction to Context

Once the level and type of instructional support that is most appropriate for a child has been identified, the next step is to match the instruction to a delivery context. There are two key ways to think about this match. The first is to identify the type of skill deficit: Is it an acquisition problem, a performance problem, or a problem of interfering behaviors (Snell & Janney, 2000)? Previously we discussed how the various levels and types of instruction could be applied to potential performance and skill deficits. A child's unique combination of preferences, mannerisms, and skill levels will, of course, ultimately determine the course of direction. In general, children with performance or fluency deficits require multiple opportunities to practice a learned skill, which is best achieved by incorporating naturally occurring social contexts as much as possible. When the natural setting does not present sufficient opportunities, then it may be necessary to modify the environment to increase and support those opportunities. Additionally, environmental modifications can encourage the use of new skills while reducing opportunities for unwanted competing behaviors. For example, if a child tends to engage in high rates of stereotypy with pens and pencils by tapping them repeatedly on a table or desk, instead of attending to individuals and activities around him or her, a cooperative learning group or play group may be created that does not include these items (e.g., focuses on gross-motor movements). Children and youth with ASD who continue to require support to master a skill sufficiently enough to engage in a successful social interactions will typically require a level of direct instruction provided through adult- or peer-mediated coaching strategies. When peer-mediated strategies are employed within natural or somewhat modified environments, children and youth have the opportunity to practice and become successful in executing their skills within the social interaction context. This facilitates generalization of new skills (acquisition), which is often a challenge for children and youth with ASD.

The second manner by which a match between context and instruction is made involves incorporating a child's strengths into social interaction contexts. In other words, a teacher would use a child's strong suit to teach a deficit area. For example, a child who excels at computer games and needs to learn how to interact with peers instead of playing alone could be taught how to take turns by playing a computer game that has timed intervals for two players with one set of controls. It is important to determine whether you will use typical instructional contexts or noninstructional contexts. An instructional context is defined as any context wherein the defining characteristics or set of interactions are based on adult instruction of an academic or functional curriculum (e.g., math, daily living skills). Noninstructional contexts are a set of interactions that are defined by the environment and activity and are typically centered around recreation or leisure activities (e.g., lunchtime, playground, computer time, quiet reading time). Although it can and should be argued that all contexts within the educational setting are geared around learning, different contexts are specific to acquisition. In contrast, other contexts involve opportunities to practice learned or alternate skills. The following two profiles highlight the importance of matching context and instruction.

Andrew is an 11-year-old boy with Asperger syndrome. He is chronologically at the fifth-grade level, but functions academically at the fourth-grade level. He enjoys his academic work a great deal and prefers to do extra work rather than go out for recess or play classroom games. However, he does not like tasks that require math skills. Andrew has functional verbal communication and frequently seeks adult support. He displays stilted, but appropriate, social skills with adults, but almost never interacts with peers, often not even acknowledging their presence. Andrew does not have significant behavioral challenges, but when frustrated, he becomes very withdrawn for long periods of time and refuses to talk to anyone.

Carey is a 15-year-old girl diagnosed with autism. She can communicate effectively using a combination of verbalizations and picture communication symbols. She seems to tolerate people well and can interact appropriately with peers one on one, but becomes inappropriately excited when more than two peers are near. Carey does not like to work independently and prefers group activities. She has learned some appropriate social skills from her teachers, but has not successfully used these skills with a variety of people or in different settings.

Based on these two profiles, Andrew would likely benefit from a small, peer-based cooperative learning group within a structured academic activity (that does not include math). He could build on his strengths, yet break patterns of isolation. Carey, on the other hand, seems to prefer highly active, recreational noninstructional activities, but she also needs to expand her core skills to peer combinations of two or more and to varied situations. Peer networks within noninstructional activities may be a logical fit for her. As with most effective instruction for students with special needs, specific determination of where, who, and how to promote peer-related social competence is based largely on individual assessment data that inform teachers about the conditions under which students demonstrate specific strengths as well as needs. Additionally, such data help pinpoint the areas of need that should be prioritized based on the discrepancy between the student's current level of functioning and the expectations of the present and future environments. By scaffolding instruction around naturally occurring opportunities or materials, teachers can build on students' strengths to enhance social interactions that set the stage for peer-related social competence.

Key Components of Effective Programming

A substantial body of literature exists on research-based social interaction practices that are effective for children and youth with ASD, many of which were highlighted in this booklet. Regardless of the exact combination of intervention and context, there are several key components of effective programming for social competence based on age level. Teachers should consider the following when creating any social competence plan or activities:

Young Elementary-Age Youth
1. Priorities should be placed on teaching the responding and maintaining behaviors that are considered essential for ongoing peer relationships. Initiations should also be taught because such behavior facilitates independence.
2. When appropriate, social cognition skills such as talking through feelings, solving problems, and interpreting motives of others should be targeted.
3. Settings should be adult structured but not controlled by adults unless goals specifically call for adult-mediated direct skill instruction. Adults should provide structure by setting rules, establishing themes, and assigning roles (DeKlyen & Odom, 1989). As children get older, teachers should have them do these three things themselves.
4. Highest levels of social interaction for young children tend to occur during free play and cleanup (Odom, Peterson, McConnell, & Ostrosky, 1990). Although these activities are less structured, they should still follow the guidelines delineated previously for adult-structured environments. Free play occurs around centers, where children play in certain areas with certain toys. Likewise, cleanup is purposeful (e.g., children must put things away, but are not shown how). Teachers need to set the rules, themes, and assign roles, and then remove themselves.
5. Research indicates that the volume of play space may be inversely correlated with amount of play. Small but adequate play

areas afford increased opportunities for peer-related social interactions.

6. Materials found to be instrumental in promoting peer interaction include simple toys that promote creativity and interaction (e.g., blocks, housekeeping materials, water toys). In contrast, high-tech toys often promote alone play.

Secondary-Age Through Adolescent Youth

1. More emphasis should be placed on the concept of friendship as children get older, and includes leisure activities and interactions.
2. Friendship is defined as an affective tie between two individuals that is mutually preferred and enjoyed. Peers with ASD and typically developing peers should be exposed to a variety of contexts in which to engage.
3. Priorities should be placed on teaching the responding and maintaining behaviors that are considered essential for ongoing peer relationships. Initiations should also be taught, but not necessarily as the primary target, unless the goal is independence.
4. Development of clear supports for students with ASD that tap into their strengths and comfort zones should be encouraged. These can include providing quantifiable information (e.g., self-monitoring data, videotaping), providing general rules, focusing on interest areas, teaching key skills (i.e., pivotal skills that are age appropriate, like "high-five"), and providing structured opportunities for reflection.
5. Peer groups and peer networks should be assisted in developing a structure and set of rules by which to live (e.g., what to say and to whom to say it when frustrated with an interaction).
6. Social cognition skills should be emphasized for both peers with ASD and nondisabled youth, including talking through feelings, solving problems, and interpreting motives of others.
7. Conversational skills should be taught, including questioning and listening skills. Analogies or metaphors (through visual representation) can represent conversations and social scripts.
8. Discussion, role playing, and processes for perspective taking should be encouraged.
9. Friendship is defined as freely choosing friends and participating in mutual and reciprocal exchanges (Stainback & Stainback, 1987).

Therefore, for secondary-age youth, teachers should provide consistent opportunities for peers to interact that may be built into school schedules (e.g., part of study hall, off-campus lunch) and include peer networks so that friendships may develop from a number of acquaintances and classmates.

References

Allen, K. E., Hart, B., Buell, J. S., Harris, F. T., & Wolf, M. M. (1964). Effects of social reinforcement on isolate behavior of a nursery school child. *Child Development, 35,* 511–518.

Asmus, J. M., Conroy, M. A., Ladwig, C. N., Boyd, B., & Sellers, J. (2004). *Social skills interview.* Unpublished document.

Bijou, S. W. (1976). *Child development: The basic stage of early childhood.* Englewood Cliffs, NJ: Prentice Hall.

Brown, W., Odom, S., & Conroy, M. (2001). An intervention hierarchy for promoting preschool children's peer interactions in naturalistic environments. *Topics in Early Childhood Special Education, 21,* 162–175.

Conroy, M. A., Asmus, J. M., Ladwig, C. N., Sellers, J., & Boyd, B. (2004). *The snapshot assessment tool.* Unpublished document.

Conroy, M. A., & Brown, W. H. (2002). Preschool children: Putting research into practice. In H. Goldstein, L. Kaczmarek, & K. M. English (Eds.), *Promoting social communication in children and youth with developmental disabilities* (pp. 211–238). Baltimore: Brookes.

DeKlyen, M., & Odom, S. L. (1989). Activity structure and social interactions with peers in developmentally integrated play groups. *Journal of Early Intervention, 13,* 342–352.

Garrison-Harrell, L. G., Kamps, D. M., & Kravitz, T. (1997). The effects of peer networks on the social and communicative behavior of students with autism. *Focus on autism and other developmental disabilities, 12*(4), 241–254.

Gray, C. (1994). *The original social story book: Social stories and comic strip conversations.* Jenison, MI: Jenison Public Schools.

Grice, H. P. (1975). Logic and conversation. In P. Cole & J. Morgan (Eds.), *Syntax and semantics* (Vol. 3; pp. 41–58). New York: Academic Press.

Haring, T. G., & Breen, C. G. (1992). A peer-mediated social network intervention to enhance the social integration of persons with moderate and severe disabilities. *Journal of Applied Behavior Analysis, 25*(2), 319–333.

Myles, B., & Simpson, R. (2001). Understanding the hidden curriculum: An essential social skill for children and youth with Asperger syndrome. *Intervention in School and Clinic, 36,* 279–286.

Odom, S. L., & McConnell, S. R. (1985). A performance-based conceptualization of social competence of handicapped preschool children: Implications for assessment. *Topics in Early Childhood Special Education, 4*(4), 1–19.

Odom, S. L., McConnell, S. R., & McEvoy, M. A. (1992). Peer-related social competence and its significance for young children with disabilities. In S. L. Odom, S. R. McConnell, & M. A. McEvoy (Eds.), *Social competence of young children with disabilities: Issues and strategies for intervention* (pp. 3–36). Baltimore: Brookes.

31

Odom, S. L., Peterson, G., McConnell, S., & Ostrosky, M. (1990). Ecobehavioral analysis of early education/specialized classroom settings and peer social interaction. *Education and Treatment of Children, 13,* 316–330.

Odom, S. L., & Strain, P. (1984). Classroom-based social skills instruction for severely handicapped preschool children. *Exceptional Children, 51,* 41–48.

Odom, S. L., & Strain, P. S. (1986). Using teacher antecedents and peer initiations to increase reciprocal social interactions of autistic children. *Journal of Applied Behavior Analysis, 19,* 59–71.

Odom, S. L., Zercher, C., Li, S., Marquart, J. M., & Sandall, S. (2004). *Social acceptance and social rejection of children with disabilities in inclusive preschool settings.* Manuscript in preparation.

Sasso, G. M. (1989, September). *Promoting social relationships in individuals with autism.* Paper presented at the meeting of the Council for Children with Behavioral Disorders, Charlotte, NC.

Sasso, G. M., Mundschenk, N. A., Melloy, K. J., & Casey, S. D. (1998). Comparison of the effects of organismic and setting variables on the social interaction behavior of children with developmental disabilities and autism. *Focus on Autism and Other Developmental Disabilities, 13,* 2–16.

Scott, J., Clark, C., & Brady, M. (2000). *Students with autism: Characteristics and instructional programming for special educators.* San Diego, CA: Singular.

Snell, M. E., & Janney, R. (2000). *Social relationships and peer support.* Baltimore: Brookes.

Stainback, S., & Stainback, W. (1987). Integration versus cooperation: A commentary on educating children with learning problems: A shared responsibility. *Exceptional Children, 54,* 66–68.

Strain, P. S., & Shores, R. E. (1977). Social reciprocity: A review of research and educational implications. *Exceptional Children, 43,* 526–530.

Vygotsky, L. S. (1978). *Mind and society: The development of higher psychological processes.* Cambridge, MA: Harvard University Press.

Child's Name Garrison

Age 6.9 years

Sex (M) F

Date of Interview 11/12/05

Interviewer Danielle

Respondent Name and Relationship to Child Ms. Raddison, Classroom Teacher

Educational Setting First-grade class at Hidden Acres School

A. Communication Strategies

1. Describe specific communication strategies (appropriate and inappropriate) used by the child (e.g., vocal speech, signs/gestures, communication boards/books, or disruptive behaviors).

   Garrison uses short phrases to communicate with peers. Occasionally, he uses gestures by pointing to things.

2. How consistently does the child use these communication strategies during social interaction opportunities with peers?

   Garrison rarely initiates to peers unless his teacher directs him to ask a peer to play.

3. How does the child respond to complex (2–3 steps) versus simple (one step) directions?

   Depending on the activity, Garrison will follow routines; however, he usually only remembers the first or last step of complex directions.

Note. From *Social Skills Interview*, by J. M. Asmus, M. A. Conroy, C. N. Ladwig, B. Boyd, & J. Sellers, 2004, unpublished document.

B. Current Social Behavior

For each social behavior, define the topography (i.e., what it looks like) and the frequency (i.e., how often the child engages in the behavior). Include both appropriate and inappropriate social behaviors (e.g., positive initiations or responses to peers/adults, negative initiations or responses to peers/adults, such as yelling, taking toys without asking) and behaviors that are likely to lead to social interactions, such as observing peers' play, responding to others' social initiations. Also indicate the times and activities during which the child is most likely to display these behaviors.

1. **Appropriate social behaviors** (e.g., gestures, verbal initiations, sharing play materials, passive acceptance, verbal gestures, walking away from peer).

Behavior	Time/Activity
a. verbal initiations	lunch, recess
b. verbal responses	following peer initiations
c.	

2. **Inappropriate social behaviors** (e.g., external may include aggression, taking toys, crying, tantrums, stereotypy; internal may include failure to approach peers who are socially interacting, failure to respond to peer initiations).

Externalizing behaviors	Internalizing behaviors
a. none	socially withdrawn
b.	won't approach peers in group activities
c.	

3. Does the child often engage in the same type of play repeatedly (e.g., with certain peers, with certain materials)? If so, identify the activities that promote different types of play (i.e., cooperative or associative).

   Yes. In the classroom, he plays with books. Outside, he plays on the swing set.

4. What medical or physical conditions, if any, does the child have that may affect his or her social behaviors (e.g., physical impairments, current medications)?

   Not applicable

5. Does the child's social behaviors and interaction skills remain constant or change depending on the activities? If it changes based on activity, identify which activities increase or decrease likelihood of social behaviors.

Increase: Music, general classroom setting

Decrease: When he gets too loud in the classroom

C. Schedule of Social Interaction Opportunities

1. Identify social times and activities (or situational factors) when the child has access to socially competent peers.

Time and Activities
Music class: Wednesday only (9:30–10:00 a.m.)
Computer time: daily in the afternoon
Lunch: daily at 11:30 a.m.
Book Area: daily at 2:15 p.m.

Situational Factors
1:1 with peer in a cooperative way
Small group of peers (2 to 3 total)
Adult-directed activity

2. Are there specific materials that increase social interactions (appropriate or inappropriate) or decrease social interactions? If so, please list them below and describe how they influence social behaviors.

Most Likely: Garrison loves to play with balloons.

Least Likely: Large group of children; noisy activity

3. Does the child have the opportunity to make choices about engaging in social interactions (e.g., with whom, what activities)? If so, when, how often, and what activities are selected? Does the child typically choose to engage with peers or adults?

Garrison can choose to interact with peers during lunch and recess, and sometimes before and after school. Typically, he will choose to engage with adults.

4. Are there other peer characteristics that make a difference in the child's display of appropriate and inappropriate social behaviors (e.g., playing with same gender peers, familiar peers, older peers, younger peers, more verbal peers)?

Garrison initiates play more with other boys in the classroom. He has a few children that are his friends, particuarly Michael and Roberto.

D. Antecedent Events That Predict Social Behavior

1. With whom is the child most and least likely to interact (include adults and peers and identify by name)?

Most Likely: *Michael at lunch and Roberto on the bus*

Least Likely: *Most of the children in the classroom*

2. Rate on the scale below the likelihood of the child engaging in an *appropriate* social interaction in the following situations.

1 = *appropriate behavior not at all likely*
5 = *appropriate behavior highly likely*

	Not at all likely				Highly likely
a. If a peer initiates the interaction?	1	(2)	3	4	5
b. If a peer responds to the child's initiation?	(1)	2	3	4	5
c. If an adult actively helps the child get engaged in play with a peer?	1	2	3	(4)	5
d. If the adult simply tells the child or peers to play with one another?	1	(2)	3	4	5
e. If the adult plans activity and child follows through and does activity?	(1)	2	3	4	5
f. If child is in a group of six or more peers playing?	(1)	2	3	4	5
g. If child is in a small group of fewer than six peers playing?	1	2	3	(4)	5
h. If the adult directs the activity?	1	2	3	(4)	5
i. If the child directs the activity?	(1)	2	3	4	5
j. If the adult is present and participating in the activity?	1	(2)	3	4	5

	Not at all likely			Highly likely	
k. If the adult is absent and disengaged from the activity?	①	2	3	4	5
l. If the peers playing are the same gender as the child?	1	2	3	④	5

3. Rate on the scale below the likelihood of the child engaging in an *inappropriate* social interaction in the following situations.

	Not at all likely			Highly likely	
a. If a peer initiates the interaction?	①	2	3	4	5
b. If a peer responds to the child's initiation?	①	2	3	4	5
c. If an adult actively helps the child get engaged in play with a peer?	①	2	3	4	5
d. If the adult simply tells the child or peers to play with one another?	①	2	3	4	5
e. If the adult plans activity and child follows through and does activity?	①	2	3	4	5
f. If child is in a group of six or more peers playing?	①	2	3	4	5
g. If child is in a small group of fewer than six peers playing?	①	2	3	4	5
h. If the adult directs the activity?	①	2	3	4	5
i. If the child directs the activity?	①	2	3	4	5
j. If the adult is present and participating in the activity?	①	2	3	4	5
k. If the adult is absent and disengaged from the activity?	①	2	3	4	5
l. If the peers playing are the same gender as the child?	①	2	3	4	5

4. Are there particular idiosyncratic situations or events not listed above that may increase or decrease the occurrence of appropriate and inappropriate social interactions (e.g., presence or absence of certain peers, types of directions, transitions, presence or absence of certain toys)?

Increase: Adult-directed or Michael-directed activities cause an increase in appropriate social interactions.

Decrease:

37

5. What one thing could or does happen that would most likely encourage or discourage the child to interact positively with peers?

Encourage: Constant verbal prompting would encourage positive interactions.

Discourage:

E. Identification of Outcomes of Appropriate and Inappropriate Social Behaviors (i.e., the functions the behaviors serve for the child in particular situations)

1. What do you think the child obtains from social interactions, whether appropriate or inappropriate (e.g., peer/adult attention, self-reinforcement, play materials)?

Garrison appears to initiate to peers to get food, a toy, the computer, or because an adult instructed him to initiate or respond.

2. What do you think the child escapes if she or he chooses not to engage in social interactions (e.g., peer/adult attention, activity, situation)?

Garrison will often withdraw to escape having to play with peers and to have more time to play by himself with toys or the computer.

3. Do appropriate or inappropriate social initiations result in successful outcomes for the child (e.g., Does she or he obtain attention or tangibles)?

Garrison will sometimes socially interact to get access to a toy he wants (e.g., book, computer).

F. Description of Interventions To Use or Avoid in Working with and Supporting This Child During Social Situations

1. What strategies used in the past have been successful at improving the child's social interactions?

Verbal prompting, consistent peers, social activities embedded into routines

2. What should be avoided that might interfere with or disrupt a social situation for this child (e.g., particular adult demands, crowded situation, noisy toys, lights)?

   Loud voices, a child crying, negative facial expressions

3. What strategies are you currently using to promote appropriate social behaviors?

   Verbal prompting

4. What strategies are you currently using to decrease inappropriate social behaviors?

   Garrison doesn't show any problem behaviors; however, he needs to learn about personal space in interacting with his peers.

5. How much does adult proximity predict the child's engagement in social interactions?

   Adult in proximity: If an adult is not near him, he will not interact.

   Adult not in proximity:

Child's Name: Garrison

Observer: Danielle

Time of Observation: 10:30 a.m.; 11:30 a.m.

Date: 12/06/05

Activity: Outdoor Play; Lunch

Type and Form of Behavior	Context and Appropriateness of Behavior	Reciprocity of Exchange	Perceived Goal of Behavior	Actual Outcome
G. initiated a request to obtain a play item; Said "hey" repeatedly to student on swing	Outside on playground swings; Socially appropriate	No peer response	To obtain tangible activity (swing)	Successful: Teacher gave G. the swing she was sitting on
G. initiated social interaction to comfort a peer; Said "Uh-oh!" repeatedly after a student was hit by the swing G. was on	Outside on playground swings; Socially appropriate	No peer response	To obtain peer attention	Unsuccessful: Peer kept walking
Peer asked G. if he wanted to play ball	During outdoor play; G. was on swings	No response from G.	Continue tangible activity (swinging) and escape peer attention	Successful: G. continued to swing
Peer asked G. if he wanted to sit at his lunch table	During lunch in the lunchroom	No response from G.	Escape peer attention	Successful: G. went and sat at another table
G. initiated social interaction by pointing and repeating a noise to a boy at his table after the boy made some noise	During lunch in the lunchroom	No peer response	To gain peer attention	Unsuccessful
Peer asked G. if he needed help with his lunch tray	During lunch in the lunchroom	G. responded by repeating the peer's request and handed him the tray; Peer took the tray and G. followed him to the cleanup counter	To obtain peer attention and assistance with task	Successful

Note. Snapshot Assessment Tool, by M. A. Conroy, J. M. Asmus, C. N. Ladwig, J. Sellers, and B. Boyd, 2004, unpublished manuscript. Used with permission. *Snapshot Assessment Tool* was adapted from "Preschool Children: Putting Research into Practice," by M. A. Conroy and W. H. Brown, 2004, in *Promoting Social Communication: Children with Developmental Disorders from Birth to Adolescence,* Baltimore: Brookes.

What happened?

_____

_____

_____

_____

What was the social error?	Who was hurt by the social error?

What should be done to correct the error?

_____

_____

_____

_____

_____

What could be done next time?

_____

_____

_____

_____

_____

_____

_____

_____

Richard L. Simpson, PhD, is professor of special education at the University of Kansas. He currently directs several federally supported projects to prepare teachers and leadership professionals for careers with children and youth with autism spectrum disorders. Simpson has also worked as a teacher of students with disabilities, psychologist, and administrator of several programs for students with autism. He is the former editor of the journal *Focus on Autism and Other Developmental Disabilities* and the author of numerous books and articles on autism spectrum disorders.

Janine Peck Stichter, PhD, is an associate professor at the University of Missouri–Columbia. Stichter conducts research in functional analysis, social skills assessment and intervention, the correlation of specific environmental variables with increases in prosocial and academic behaviors, and the development and implementation of school-based curriculum for students with autism spectrum disorders. She has published more than 30 peer-reviewed articles and has made more than 50 national presentations on research related to autism and behavior challenges. Stichter serves on numerous editorial boards, including *Focus on Autism and Other Developmental Disorders* and *Journal of Positive Behavior Interventions.*

Maureen A. Conroy is an associate professor in the Department of Special Education at the University of Florida. She received her PhD from Vanderbilt University with an emphasis in early childhood special education and behavior disorders. Conroy has been in the field of special education for more than 25 years as a teacher of young children with autism spectrum disorders, parent trainer, administrator of early intervention programs, and university faculty member. Her research interests are the functional assessment and analysis of problem behaviors, assessment and intervention of social skills in young children with autism, and setting events.